"There is still a lot worth fighting for"

Dame Jane Goodall, Ethologist.

With thanks to Professor Anastazia Banaszak, lead coral photobiologist at Universidad Nacional Autonoma De Mexico and her incredibly dedicated team.
We thank you with all our hearts for all the work you are doing to protect the coral.

Copyright ©

Ian Derry

Published May 2024

All rights reserved. No part of this book may be reproduced or transmitted by any means, except as permitted by UK law or the author. For licensing requests please contact ian@ianderry.com.

THE CORAL BABIES

A STORY OF HOPE

Written by Ian Derry

Illustrations by Sam Scott

The story of a baby coral named Hope.

I came across this story of Hope while I was making a film called BENEATH THE SURFACE - The Fight For Corals.

We travelled to Mexico where I met Ania and her incredible team of scientists. This is where I was introduced to the amazing story of a coral baby named Hope.

We saw many incredible initiatives that can hopefully combat global warming and future proof our corals, but we also saw some devastation that reduced our crew to tears.

The one thing I understood from all the experts involved was they all had hope. But they cannot do it alone, they need filmmakers, they need communities globally, business globally, education and pressure on those who continue to be part of the problem not the solution.

No matter what age, young or old, we all need to come together as individuals to try to save our planet for the future.

Ian

Marine biologist Ania is sitting on a long white sandy beach in the warm Mexican sunshine, she is feeling sad. She has always had a deep love for the ocean but she knows it is in trouble and in need of some urgent help.

Manatee Bay FL

Global warming has caused record high sea temperatures that are destroying the world's corals. Ania knows that without these corals and their delicate ecosystems the planet is heading towards a very dangerous situation.

Without coral there will be no fish. Without fish there will be much less food. Without food some people will have to leave their communities and travel to other areas to feed their families.

Ania and her small team work tirelessly to save the dying coral reef and they decide to try something new. If they collect the sperm and eggs from the few healthy corals that still exist in the ocean, maybe they could breed them in the safety of her laboratory.

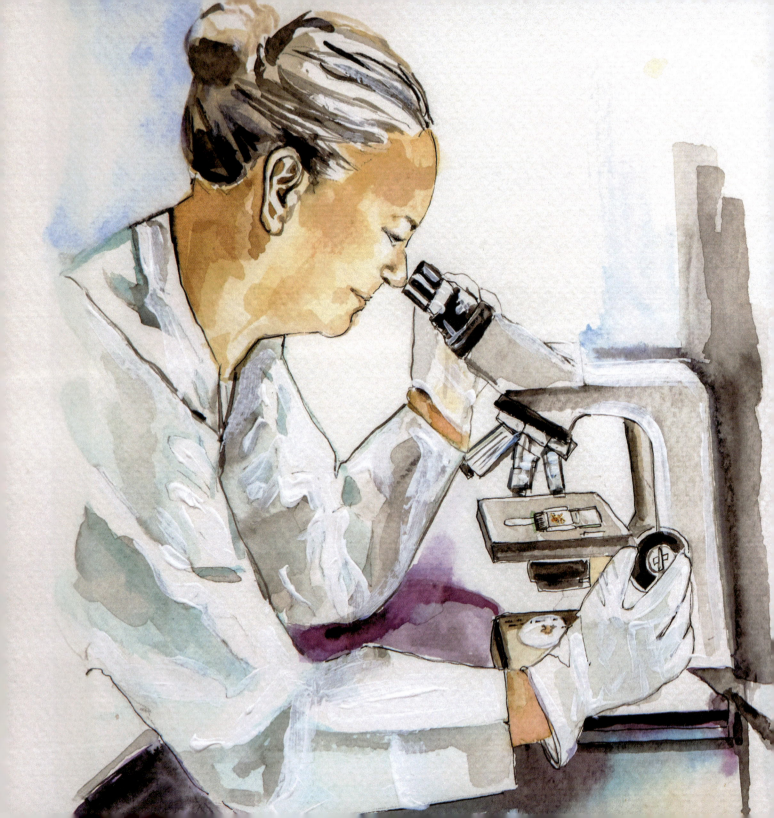

It's a difficult process as coral only breed once a year on a particular lunar cycle but Ania would not give up. It took time but miraculously one day Ania looked through her microscope and saw she had created a tiny coral baby that she named Hope. Hope was born from the love of the ocean and Ania hoped that this could be the key to bringing the ocean back to life.

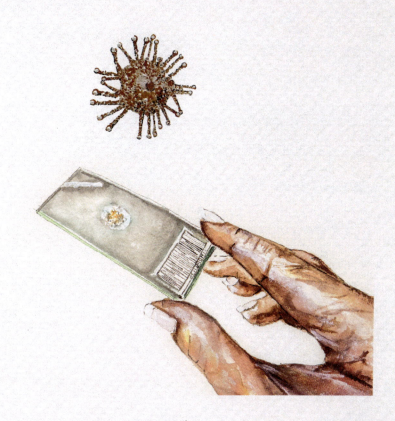

Ania loved Hope like a parent loves their child. She cared for Hope every day, ensuring the little coral baby was healthy and strong. She had to feed the baby coral and keep its water at the correct temperature. Hope began to grow in the safety of the laboratory.

The news of Hope's growth spread, and many people became excited about the possibility of saving the coral reefs. Ania and her team of passionate helpers prepared to transplant Hope back into the dying ocean.

It was a colossal challenge, fraught with difficulties and doubts along the way. But Ania was strong, believing in Hope's potential to make a significant difference.

Finally, Hope was gently placed back into the water on the seabed. Everyone waited anxiously, hoping for a miracle. Weeks and months passed, and initially it seemed like Hope was struggling amidst the vast devastation. Hope looked so small, so lonely and vulnerable. Ania would lie awake at night thinking of the tiny baby out in the huge ocean.

Then, a miraculous event occurred. Hope managed to create tiny coral babies of its own! They spread and grew, breathing life back into the ocean's floor. Ania's dream was beginning to come true!

The once-barren ocean beds began to transform into vibrant and lively ecosystems as new corals grew, and more sea creatures returned. Hope's legacy lived on through generations of new corals, reminding everyone that determination and love could bring beauty and life back, even in the darkest times.

The ocean is a magical garden, and with a little hope, it can thrive once again.

Printed in Great Britain
by Amazon